Harriet Tubman

HERO of the UNDERGROUND RAILROAD

by LORI MORTENSEN
illustrated by FRANCES MOORE

PICTURE WINDOW BOOKS
Minneapolis, Minnesota

Special thanks to our advisers for their expertise:

Professor Lois Brown
Mount Holyoke College
South Hadley, Massachusetts

Susan Kesselring, M.A., Literacy Educator
Rosemount–Apple Valley–Eagan (Minnesota) School District

Editor: Nick Healy
Designer: Nathan Gassman
Page Production: Melissa Kes
Associate Managing Editor: Christianne Jones
The illustrations in this book were created digitally.
Photo Credit: Library of Congress, page 3

Picture Window Books
5115 Excelsior Boulevard, Suite 232
Minneapolis, MN 55416
877-845-8392
www.picturewindowbooks.com

Printed in the United States of America.

Library of Congress Cataloging-in-Publication Data
Mortensen, Lori, 1955-
Harriet Tubman : hero of the Underground Railroad / by Lori Mortensen ;
illustrated by Frances Moore.
p. cm. — (Biographies)
Includes bibliographical references and index.
Audience: Grades K-3.
ISBN-13: 978-1-4048-3103-2 (library binding)
ISBN-10: 1-4048-3103-7 (library binding)
1. Tubman, Harriet, 1820?-1913—Juvenile literature. 2. Slaves—United States—
Biography—Juvenile literature. 3. African American women—Biography—Juvenile
literature. 4. Underground railroad—Juvenile literature. 5. Antislavery movements—
United States—History—19th century—Juvenile literature. I. Moore, Frances, ill.
II. Title.
E444.T82M667 2007
973.7'115092—dc22
[B]   2006027225

Harriet Tubman was one of the bravest people in American history. She lived at a time when many black people were held in slavery. Harriet believed black people should be free. After escaping slavery, she risked her life to help free many other slaves.

This is the story of *Harriet Tubman.*

Around 1820, Harriet was born on a plantation in Maryland. She and her family were forced to live as slaves. While their master lived in a big house, they lived in a small cabin. It did not have any windows or furniture. The floor was dirt.

Harriet did not get to play like most other children. She had to work. She didn't even get to live with her family. When she was about 5 years old, her master started sending her to work for other families. At one home, she cleaned the house and took care of a baby. The mistress said if the baby cried, Harriet would get whipped. The baby did cry. The mistress kept her promise.

One day, Harriet got into trouble for taking some sugar. She was 7 years old and had never had such a treat. The mistress saw Harriet with her hand in the sugar bowl. She chased the girl with a whip.

Harriet ran away from her angry mistress. She hid in a pigpen for five days. She had to fight the pigs for food scraps. Finally, she got so hungry that she went back to the house. She knew she would be punished.

Harriet survived her difficult childhood. She grew into a strong young woman. When Harriet was 24, she married John Tubman. John was free. But marrying John did not make Harriet free. She later decided she would be free or die trying.

Several years later, Harriet's master died. Harriet soon heard that she would be sold to another slaveholder. She could not bear the thought.

Harriet ran away. She went to the home of a friendly white woman. The woman gave Harriet a slip of paper with two names on it. This was Harriet's first "ticket" on the Underground Railroad.

The Underground Railroad was not a real railroad. It was a series of homes. The people at these homes helped slaves escape. The homes were called stations. Slaves were called passengers. The people who guided them were called conductors.

At the first station, a woman told Harriet to sweep
the porch. This worried Harriet. But then she realized the task was a way to
keep her safe. It made her look like one of the workers. After dark, Harriet
climbed into a wagon and hid under a sack. She stayed there until a man
drove her to the next stop on the Underground Railroad.

Most of the time, Harriet traveled on her own. During the day, people hid her in barns, attics, and haystacks. At night, Harriet had to get to the next stop by herself. She waded through muddy rivers and watched the North Star. Harriet knew if she followed it, the star would lead her north to freedom.

After traveling 130 miles (208 kilometers) on foot, Harriet reached a city in the North—Philadelphia, Pennsylvania. For the first time in her life, Harriet was free. There was no slavery in the North. Still, runaway slaves like Harriet weren't totally safe. They had to avoid slave catchers who wanted to return them to the South.

Harriet returned to Maryland 19 times and led 300 slaves to freedom. She was a conductor on the Underground Railroad. She was never captured, and she never lost a passenger. Many slaves called her Moses because she led people to freedom, just like Moses led people to freedom in the Bible.

In 1861, the Civil War began. Harriet helped the Northern Army. Alongside troops from the North, she returned to the South, where most fighting took place. She washed clothes, cooked, and nursed wounded soldiers. The men she cared for included African-American soldiers. They were members of a famous group. They were called the Massachusetts 54th Regiment.

Harriet became a spy and a soldier, too. She crossed enemy lines and learned many important things. One time, she discovered where the enemy had planted torpedoes along a river. Later, she returned with 300 soldiers and removed the bombs.

When the war ended, Harriet returned home to New York. She never stopped helping others. She founded a home for homeless African-American people. She built a school for children who needed help. And she worked for women's right to vote.

Harriet died on March 10, 1913. She was 93. Soldiers saluted and flags waved at her funeral. It was a fitting way to honor the woman who risked her life so others could be free.

The Life of Harriet Tubman

1820	Born in Bucktown, Maryland; the exact date is unknown
1835	Injured by an iron weight thrown at her head
1844	Married John Tubman
1849	Escaped slavery on the Underground Railroad
1850	Returned to Maryland and began freeing other slaves
1857	Rescued her parents from slavery
1869	Married Nelson Davis
1888	Widowed when Nelson Davis died
1913	Died in Auburn, New York, on March 10 at age 93

Did You Know?

- Harriet's given name was Araminta Ross. Her family called her "Minty" when she was young. When she was older, she took her mother's first name.

- When Harriet was about 15, she saw a slave running away and refused to stop him. The master got angry and threw an iron weight, which hit Harriet in the head. The injury almost killed her. For the rest of her life, Tubman suffered headaches, and a scar on her head marked the place of the wound.

- If a slave wanted to give up while on the Underground Railroad, Harriet was known to aim her pistol at him or her and say, "You'll go on, or die." The slaves always agreed to go on. Harriet could not allow slaves to turn back. If they did, they would risk everyone's safety on the Underground Railroad.

- John Tubman did not want to go North with Harriet when she escaped slavery. Harriet later returned to Maryland to rescue family members, including her parents. On one trip, she found out John had married another woman.

- The Underground Railroad may have gotten its name when a runaway slave swam across the Ohio River in 1831. By the time his master got to the other side, the slave had vanished. The master said that he escaped so quickly that "he must have gone on an underground road."

- In 1978, Harriet became the first African-American woman to be honored on a U.S. postage stamp. She was also pictured leading slaves to freedom on a U.S. stamp in 1995.

Glossary

Civil War (1861–1865) — the battle between states in the North and the South that led to the end of slavery in the United States

conductor — someone who is in charge of a railroad car, bus, or streetcar

master — a man in charge of a plantation or owner of a slave

mistress — a woman in charge of a household or owner of a slave

Moses — a person in the Bible who led his people out of slavery in Egypt

plantation — a large farm where crops are raised by people who live there

slavery — the practice of owning people; these people are slaves and are not free

To Learn More

At the Library

Gayle, Sharon. *Harriet Tubman and the Freedom Train.* New York: Aladdin, 2003.

Mara, Wil. *Harriet Tubman.* New York: Children's Press, 2003.

Martin, Michael. *Harriet Tubman and the Underground Railroad.* Mankato, Minn.: Capstone Press, 2005.

Rau, Dana Meachen. *Harriet Tubman.* Mankato, Minn.: Compass Point Books, 2001.

On the Web

FactHound offers a safe, fun way to find Web sites related to this book. All of the sites on FactHound have been researched by our staff.

1. Visit *www.facthound.com*

2. Type in this special code: 1404831037

3. Click on the FETCH IT button.

Your trusty FactHound will fetch the best sites for you!

Index

Look for all of the books in the Biographies series:

Abraham Lincoln: Lawyer, President, Emancipator

Benjamin Franklin: Writer, Inventor, Statesman

Frederick Douglass: Writer, Speaker, and Opponent of Slavery

George Washington: Farmer, Soldier, President

Harriet Tubman: Hero of the Underground Railroad

Martin Luther King Jr.: Preacher, Freedom Fighter, Peacemaker

Pocahontas: Peacemaker and Friend to the Colonists

Sally Ride: Astronaut, Scientist, Teacher

Susan B. Anthony: Fighter for Freedom and Equality

Thomas Edison: Inventor, Scientist, and Genius